A gift as a thank you!

The cryptocurrency world is a fast moving world.

If you want to stay up-to-date, please check out the author's website:

www.aboutcryptocurrencies.net

Here you will find the latest cryptocurrencies news gathered from around the world and updated multiple times per day.

Sign-up for the 'Daily Crypto News' and receive the electronic version of the officially published book:

'Bitcoin: What is Bitcoin?'

for free as a thank you for buying this book.

- So go to *www.aboutcryptocurrencies.net*
- sign up
- get the 'Bitcoin: What is Bitcoin?' as a thank you.

And you know, only make educated decisions!

Yours sincerely,

Johan von Amsterdam

© **Copyright 2018 by Johan von Amsterdam - All rights reserved.**

This document is geared towards providing exact and reliable information in regards to the topic and issue covered. The publication is sold with the idea that the publisher is not required to render accounting, officially permitted, or otherwise, qualified services. If advice is necessary, legal or professional, a practiced individual in the profession should be ordered.

- From a Declaration of Principles which was accepted and approved equally by a Committee of the American Bar Association and a Committee of Publishers and Associations.

In no way is it legal to reproduce, duplicate, or transmit any part of this document in either electronic means or in printed format. Recording of this publication is strictly prohibited and any storage of this document is not allowed unless with written permission from the publisher. All rights reserved.

The information provided herein is stated to be truthful and consistent, in that any liability, in terms of inattention or otherwise, by any usage or abuse of any policies, processes, or directions contained within is the solitary and utter responsibility of the recipient reader. Under no circumstances will any legal responsibility or blame be held against the publisher for any reparation, damages, or monetary loss due to the information herein, either directly or indirectly.

Respective authors own all copyrights not held by the publisher.

The information herein is offered for informational purposes solely, and is universal as so. The presentation of the information is without contract or any type of guarantee assurance.

The trademarks that are used are without any consent, and the publication of the trademark is without permission or backing by the trademark owner. All trademarks and brands within this book are for clarifying purposes only and are the owned by the owners themselves, not affiliated with this document.

Monero versus Bitcoin

The battle of the cryptocurrencies

Johan von Amsterdam

Introduction

Cryptocurrencies are a revolution, one that promises change not only to the financial markets but also to other industries and sectors. Their development has brought to the world a paradigm shift in the way things are done, a shift which is shaking up the status quo as well as the way issues are thought of and solved. The ingenuity behind the development of cryptocurrencies exudes both brilliance and the need to harness the power of technology to take the world to the next level.

These forms of currency have brought promise and hope to individuals worldwide; their promises embedded in words such as decentralization – the elimination of third parties such as banks from the transaction table –, low to zero transaction costs, high speed transactions and high security. Most people have only been made aware of the above strengths akin to the new technology.

However, a critique of this promises has yet to be done. If done, the critique would have raised one question: do these promises actually hold?

A look into the purchase of or transactions using Bitcoin paints a different picture as compared to the previously mentioned narrative. The picture is made dim by the realization that both purchasing Bitcoin and carrying out transactions is not entirely free. There exist both inherent as well as exogenous costs accruing to the user. As such, the question now shifts from whether transactions are free to how much do they actually cost? Furthermore, are they cheaper or more expensive as compared to the traditional banking system and if so, by how much?

This is not the case for Bitcoin alone. Other cryptocurrencies face similar challenges when trying to meet the expectations which the market has already hyped up. One such cryptocurrency is Monero, a top contender within the cryptocurrency market by market capitalization.

Monero presents a new realm to the cryptocurrency space – one discussed in the book – and is building on it to dominate the market. The latter has been the source of the coin's popularity among players within this space. However, not many people understand how it functions nor how it differs from other cryptocurrencies, especially Bitcoin. Moreover, with so many cryptocurrencies coming up in the market, the question on whether the difference is merely structural or one based on the ideology behind the formation of the coin and how this will influence the fulfilment of the promises made by the developers of the coin also lingers.

This book will answer the above questions and more.

The book will begin by shedding some light on cryptocurrencies and how they are expected to revolutionize the dynamics of global business. Here, the answer to the ever-so-debated question on the difference between digital money and cryptocurrencies will also be answered elaborately. It will, however, have an incline towards Bitcoin and Monero, trying to compare and contrast the two cryptocurrencies before finally detailing how users can benefit from their use in different settings. Eventually, a candid assessment of how the two are expected to fulfil their promises to the market will be given and its review done.

Over the course of this read, we will unravel the mystery surrounding cryptocurrencies, debunk its myths and provide in-depth information as to their future.

Table of Contents

Introduction

Table of Contents

1. **Real world examples**
2. **Bitcoin**
3. **Monero**
4. **The Battle of the Cryptocurrencies**
5. **How to buy?**
6. **Storing Cryptocurrencies**
7. **Epilogue**
8. **Conclusion**

1. Real world examples

It is true that money has evolved over time.

The evolution of money dates back to a period before recorded history had taken root. However, the oldest recorded encounter between human beings and money occurs during the era of batter trade – a time when people exchanged goods for other goods which were deemed to be of the same value. However, the use of this form of money brought with it some complexities – such as the lack of double coincidence, indivisibility of some good, difficulty in making deferred payments and lack of an objective measure of value etc. – which in turn led to the formation of commodity money, metallic money, paper money, fiat money and plastic money.

The use of the above as money eventually raised a fundamental question: was money defined by its form or by its function – was it defined by the material of worth such as gold which was used as a medium of exchange or by the fact that that material was accepted as the medium of exchange?

Economists argued over the definition of money for a long time – specifically on whether it is defined by its form or function – and they eventually decided that the function of money as a medium of exchange was what gave money its significance. Its form, such as paper or metals, was merely meant to ensure the above role was achieved (this will be important when we get to cryptocurrencies).

Furthermore, over the course of the 20th century, the emergence of fiat money begun. This was a new form of currency which, rather than being backed by an item of value, was backed by the belief that a larger body was backing up the value of the paper of coin used in the exchange. In most cases, this form of money was backed by governments though initially banks and other such institutions – mostly large institutions – had some power in backing such currencies. For this form of money to be accepted, the people using it to trade had to believe in its value being as depicted on the coin or note – the most used forms of fiat money.

From the above, two main ideas arise: the fact that money was defined by its function rather than its form as well as the idea that the value of a currency was derived from the belief that the value on it was its actual value – this may or may not be backed by a financial institution or government. It is upon this backdrop that cryptocurrencies were formed.

1.1. Cryptocurrencies

1.1.1. Cryptography

Well, cryptocurrencies are the newest form of money in the market. By definition, cryptocurrencies are assets which are used as means of exchange – however, unlike other assets, they derive their name from the fact that they have their security as well as their functionality based on cryptography.

A rudimentary definition of the term would be that cryptography is the art of writing and solving codes. Without going into the technical details, the cryptography is based mainly on math and through it, other algorithms and protocols are enabled.

However, for readers with a more technical understanding of the term, cryptography has been synonymous with encryption – techniques which are used to secure information from getting to third parties during communication – for the longest time. Encryption would convert sensible information into 'nonsense' with the help of computers. This was achieved through a process known as encoding – which was carried out by the computer which sent information – after which the recipient's computer would decode it.

The system since morphed and with the help of computational works, new forms of cryptography emerged. It was during this evolution period that the cryptographic hash function emerged.

The hash function is an exemplary way of encoding. It works through a simple principle, take in whatever data has been provided and put it in your own wording. As such, the data provided to the computer is converted into a series of fixed-size string of alphanumeric characters. This, for those with a rudimentary understanding, means that a word such as 'window' may be converted into an alphanumeric such as '43KI9CJ8'. The alphanumeric value defined above is known by many names: checksum (https://en.wikipedia.org/wiki/Checksum), digital fingerprint or merely hashes.

As such, this function converts data of any size using a hashing algorithm – known here as the hash function but described in detail later in this article – into output with a specific size (such as 256 bits).

These hash values are stored in tables. Therefore, when the computer goes through the different hash values, it then evaluates which text this hash was obtained from in a similar fashion as matching two similar characters on a table. As a result, it is a rule that no two texts, even if similar, should have the same cryptographic hash – known as cryptographic hash collisions – as a hacker may find the pattern and use it to evaluate the hash function used.

With this in mind, we can now work our way up to the system used by cryptocurrencies.

In cryptocurrencies, information from transactions in aggregated into blocks – this will be discussed in detail later in this text – and each block is assigned its own hash value. There exists a genesis block – the very first block that was formed – to which other blocks are tied. This block receives the first hash value in the chain. Thence, any block which is formed takes part of the hash value of its predecessor.

This being the case, all blocks formed after the genesis block will therefore have part of the hash from the genesis block. Furthermore, the content from this block cannot be altered given that alteration of this content would mean that even the hash functions would need to be altered – mainly because the content apportioned to that hash function has changed therefore the hash function cannot be mapped to this new content.

Upon this backdrop, in order to verify a transaction, computers on the decentralized network – nodes – would need to verify that the hash value from a specific block is tied to the hash value from its predecessor. If this is the case, then the blockchain network is stable. This very concept is what makes the entire blockchain network among the most secure networks available. This is because anyone wishing to change part of the block would need to alter the hash values of that block as well as that of all the blocks that succeed it. Furthermore, they need to do this while having higher computing power than the nodes within the network – as all nodes have to accept that this change has been made to a block. If the nodes have more computing power, they end up outperforming the attacker, eventually leading to the state prior to the hack. This makes nearly impossible – technically it is impossible – for a single hacker to change anything within the blockchain system.

However, this is not the only way cryptography works as digital signatures also play a role.

In simple terms, digital signatures are similar to handwritten signatures, as they prove that a certain individual actually carried out a transaction, except for the fact that they are held and operated on digitally. This is the case with web browsers which send digital signatures to the recipient's computers to verify that they are indeed from the authentic source.

For cryptocurrencies, these signatures come in two forms: public keys and private keys. These are sets of values which have an association with each other courtesy of some mathematical function. In most cases, these keys are 64-bit alphanumeric strings, similar to that of the hash.

Public keys ensure that people within the network can receive money or other information from the other players within the network. This key is available publicly. Private keys on the other hand aren't available publicly. This is because they are meant to ensure that the transaction emanates only from the account of the holder of the coins. This key is used to 'sign off' any transaction carried out by the user so as to ensure that the recipient can verify that the amount came from a specific user.

The signature from the keys doesn't change. Therefore, when the transactions are aggregated into a block, the signatures as well as the amounts tied to those signatures – courtesy of carrying out transactions – are assessed so as to ensure they do not change once that block is confirmed. This ensures transactions are recorded as are.

All in all, cryptocurrencies have found their grounding within cryptography. The technology (cryptocurrencies) have become synonymous with hashing and digital signatures with good reason. However, these are only the basis on which the technology works. The real technology on which cryptocurrencies are based is known as the blockchain.

1.1.2. The Blockchain System

The entire cryptocurrency system works on the blockchain platform. This platform is a decentralized and distributed ledger[1] system in which the transactions that occur within a specific period are recorded and bundled up into a block[2] and recorded.

The notion of decentralization stems from the fact that there is no single body which governs the transactions carried out on the network (which is unlike modern transactions which are governed by banks or service providers such as Visa). This, according to the founder of this system – Satoshi Nakamoto – was meant to ensure that the power of transactions was given back to the people rather than to huge corporations which stand to benefit greatly from holding people's money.

---

[1] A ledger is a book (traditionally) or system in which transactions are recorded and stored in order for the accountants to refer to when consolidating accounts or for auditors to refer to during audits.
[2] A block is a group of transactions which have been bundled together.

Moreover, the distributed ledger stems from the fact that once transactions are validated, the blocks are shared with all the nodes within the system. This ensures that all the nodes store the blockchain data such that there is not a single computer that is said to be the store of all the information. This goes a long way in furthering the concept of decentralization.

The system works on the principle that information contained within a block cannot be altered and that the block is assigned a hash value linked to that of its predecessor. in order for transactions to be recorded, the entire network of nodes – computers around the globe connected to a network which validates the cryptographic hash – need to decipher the cryptographic hash and move on to decipher the next block. A transaction is considered authentic when the nodes move to decipher the next block, at which point that block is stored within the blockchain.

The system is also programmed to read the longest chain as the correct one. Therefore, given that the entire chain of blocks stems from the genesis block and has part of the harsh from this block, generally the nodes will read this chain as the correct chain. Any additions to the blockchain will generally be added on to the longest chain and all the nodes will receive the new blocks to their systems upon their approval. This also explains why cryptocurrencies are said to be decentralized – courtesy of the nodes – while also explaining how the security of the entire blockchain is ensured – attackers need to have higher computing power to form a chain other than the longest one and get it accepted by the entire network.

However, questions arise: how do we therefore maintain the stability of the network or compensate the owners for all the nodes for keeping the network stable?

To answer the first question, the nodes are compensated based on a proof of work mechanism.

Proof of work is a mechanism/concept which was first designed to operate for Bitcoin. Its designer – Satoshi Nakamoto – meant it to be the forerunner to a decentralized economy with peer to peer payment systems.

The proof of work concept is one where the nodes have to continuously 'work' to solve the cryptographic hash problem. In this case, the work means that the nodes, having been pre-installed with the cryptocurrency's program, need to keep solving for the cryptographic hash problem for all new blocks generated. With an average of one block being generated per 10 minutes or about 144 blocks per day, the nodes need to ensure that each of these blocks is both solved for and added to the longest chain. This means that every time the nodes are working towards both ensuring that the blocks which are generated are added to the system with complete and accurate transactions and in the process ensure that the entire system is secure.

Over time, especially due to the exponential increase in the number of coins released, the mining process becomes harder. Numerically, with every 2,016 blocks created, the difficulty level required in mining is adjusted. This adjustment is based on several factors: the number of blocks mined, the number of nodes which took part in the mining process and the time taken to hash the 2,016 blocks. Over time, the difficulty level for most cryptocurrencies has been increasing as more and more miners get into the network.

This has led to more powerful systems being used to carry out mining. Initially, all that was needed was a CPU (Central Processing Unit), however, this transformed to GPUs (Graphics Processing Units) then to FPGAs (Field-Programmable Gate Arrays). Eventually, mining specific computers known as ASICs (Application-Specific Integrated Circuits) were created in order to ensure that miners had sufficient power to carry out mining effectively. Their creation made the previous three hardware options obsolete unless they were pooled together in a group.

These machines, however, have a major drawback. In order to mine, the electricity costs incurred are quite high. It is estimated that the cost of electricity attributable to mining cryptocurrencies – specifically Bitcoin – stands at about $5,000 per coin or approximately $200 per day. With such high costs seen within the network, miners require to make higher margins to offset these costs, a factor which brings us to our next question: how are node owners compensated for keeping the network stable?

In a bid to ensure decentralization is effective, the nodes within the network receive some compensation for their role of securing the network. This compensation comes in form of coins which are released to the network upon the completion of specific tasks – these tasks mainly entail the deciphering of a certain number of blocks within the network: once these blocks have been deciphered, the owners are compensated. Given this, the owners of the computers within this chain are referred to as miners.

For miners, the additional coin is meant to offset for their loss in money courtesy of electricity costs. Given the high amount of electricity consumed during the mining process, the miners use the coins received as a payoff for the high costs incurred in both the acquisition of the machinery used in mining as well as the resources used in the mining process, key being electricity.

The number of coins released, however, has slowly been reducing over time. Initially, the compensation stood at 50 coins for the first 210,000 blocks formed and this number keeps halving every time the number of blocks double. This, coupled with the fact that the number of miners has increased significantly over time, means that each coin released to the market now has to be split between the miners based on their computational power – hashing power – which makes the reward much smaller for new entrants than it was for their forerunners. However, given that the value of the coins in also increasing during this period, the gains made from its increased value may offset the small size of reward currently being received.

With all the above intricacies akin to cryptocurrencies, they seem to be a significant leap into the future of payments. With the 'entire world' being part of the validation process and the transactions being limited to peer to peer, there is a lot to benefit from when using them as a payment mechanism. Furthermore, the fact that the payments are available via a digital front makes it more convenient using cryptocurrencies.

1.1.3. Digital Currencies Versus Cryptocurrencies

Based on the above, it would be fair to conclude that cryptocurrencies can be said to be digital currencies – given the space they operate within. However, do the two have the same meaning? Can one be equivocated for the other?

The answer is no.

While it is true that cryptocurrencies are digital currencies, not all digital currencies are cryptocurrencies. By definition, digital currencies are forms of money which exist only in digital form – thus making cryptocurrencies digital currencies – however, such currency maintains the characteristics of fiat money. The main difference between digital currency and fiat money is the state in which it is held (cash versus electronic). Mostly, digital currencies are held through service providers such as PayPal, Skrill and Google Wallet and these services are enabled by the internet.

In contrast, cryptocurrencies derive their name from the fact that they are based on cryptography and operate based on this system. These currencies, however, operate on the digital space, making them all digital currencies despite there being some contrasts.

Unlike cryptocurrency, digital currency does not have a decentralized system backing the flow of funds. Rather, the system is manned by a centralized body – mostly a company – and the funds are deemed to be secure based on the security protocols that the body puts in place. Furthermore, the peer to peer element does not exist as money sent from one person to the next has to go through the service provider – for the transaction cost to be calculated and deducted – before it gets to the recipient.

While this payment method (PayPal) may take a much shorter period to be completed as compared to cryptocurrencies, the transaction costs may lead to more people preferring cryptocurrencies over PayPal. With the advancement in cryptocurrencies – such as the implementation of the Segregated Witness protocol and lightning networks, transactions will end up being much faster and this will necessitate a shift from digital currencies to cryptocurrencies. This shift, we expect, will be driven by the appreciation of the blockchain technology by the general public, a move which will propel the world to the next currency phase.

The advancements in money, as seen above, have been quite significant. With the world moving forward at a high rate, we decided to take a look at how two cryptocurrencies are driving this agenda across the globe.

2. Bitcoin

2.1. Introduction

The evolution of money did not stop with fiat money. Everyday more and more people device ways to make money serve its purpose as a method of exchange. This process has been characterized by tremendous hurdles especially from central governments which believe they will lose control of the financial system – which is their tool of enforcing monetary policy within the economy. However, the fact that money draws its value from its acceptance by the community has come to overshadow these hurdles.

Cryptocurrencies are the breakthrough which exemplified this and their forerunner, Bitcoin, became the excellent exemplar. Through this system, a shift in modern economics is about to be driven. Over the next section of this book, we will evaluate how this is the case as well as the benefits that will accrue the holders of this cryptocurrency moving forward.

2.2. History of Bitcoin

The history of Bitcoin is the history of cryptocurrency. It can be traced back to a document which was published in 2008 by an anonymous developer only known by their pseudo name: Satoshi Nakamoto – shortly after the global financial crisis.

The above was driven by the realization that the management in the top financial institutions, during the financial crisis period, suffered from moral hazard[3] and this led to institutions greatly risking funds belonging to individuals thus affecting their livelihoods adversely upon the stock market collapse. Therefore, this new system provided a new means to remove the power from financial institutions and place it back to the owners of the money. This also had the added benefit of cutting transaction costs associated with having an intermediary down to zero or near zero.

The paper in question was titled 'Bitcoin: The Peer-to-Peer Electronic Cash System'.

In it was information on a new form of exchange system that utilized the computational power of different computers across the globe to bring together a cash exchange system that would effectively eliminate intermediaries. This system harnessed the power of new technology dubbed 'blockchain'. Blockchain was to be a revolution to the financial industry. As earlier defined, a block is a set of transactions that have been grouped together. Based on the latter, a blockchain is therefore a chain of blocks.

2.2.1. The Decentralized and Distributed Network

The design of the blockchain system places more weight on the longest chain – given that this chain is most likely the most

---

[3] The principal/agent problem whereby the agent acts in a manner only to serve their own interests (such as taking up high risk using the agent's money without assessing its implications on the agent) especially in a situation where they presume themselves 'insured' by the fact that they can be bailed out by a larger body such as a government.

accepted chain. Therefore, as more blocks are formed, the longer the blockchain gets and effectively, the more secure the network is[4].

Satoshi made it such that in order for a player to become a node within the chain, they needed to download the entire system onto their computers. Once you had it, every node received a copy of the accepted blocks onto their computer – which gave the system its name as a distributed ledger. The above, coupled with the fact that the blockchain system was decentralized – not governed by a single body or institution – meant that all players within the network had access to the financial transactions from the network.

This has been the reason behind the network's growth from about 876 megabytes in the first quarter of 2012 to its current size of over 149 gigabytes.

2.2.2. The Mining Architecture

Satoshi's concept of a proof of work system is in itself a brilliant idea deduced from the basic concept of money: as more and more people accept it as a means of exchange, the more it meets its role and being this means of exchange. Satoshi's expectation was that this would hold for Bitcoin (as well as for other

---

[4] This is based on the initial paper whereby Satoshi wrote that as the network grew, it would require that the computational power of the hacker be higher than that of the whole network for them to hack it. For a much larger network, the probability of this fell exponentially with each new block thus effectively making the blockchain a secure network in itself.

cryptocurrencies which came after it) since its popularity among people – especially during the time of the global financial crisis – would rise quite fast and this dream came fruition soon after.

2.2.2.1. History

To enforce this, Satoshi used an already elaborate program: the secure hashing algorithm (SHA).

The secure hashing algorithm was created by the United States National Security Agency (NSA). It was designed to be a set of cryptographic hash functions based initially on Merkle–Damgård structure. Initially, the NSA had built a SHA-1 algorithm – which was the forerunner to all such algorithms – but the quick advancements within this field led to more complex and dynamic algorithms being developed leading to the development of the SHA-2. From this algorithm came the SHA-224, SHA-256, SHA-384, SHA-512 and others.

The transition was attributable to a key characteristic of hashing – hashes were meant follow the no collision attribute. Given that secure hashing algorithms are designed to ensure security, any vulnerability to this system – especially one pertaining the collision attribute – needed to be assessed. As such, both algorithms were tested for this.

Based on this, it was concluded that collision – previously defined as the ability for two inputs to generate the same hash – was possible for any hashing algorithm, however, the probability of collision differed between different algorithms. Upon testing, the results showed that the SHA-1 algorithm was more prone to collision unlike the SHA-2.

This vulnerability played a key role in the removal of the SHA-1 algorithm from key web browsers back in January 2017 and paved the way for the entry of SHA-2 into the market. Since then, SHA-2 has become the gold standard within the cryptography field and has come to support major corporations in their endeavour to encode their clients' credentials.

2.2.2.2. Bitcoin and SHA-2

With such trust having been placed in the SHA-2 hashing algorithm, it came as no surprise when Satoshi selected the SHA-256 as the algorithm of choice. Users of the Bitcoin system were meant to download the package and run this algorithm on the different blocks which were created. The hashing algorithm was tailored in a way to ensure that a unique hash was created for every block, however, due to its structure, newer blocks could have part of the characteristics of the previous hash.

In the case of Bitcoin, the transactions would be bundled together every 10 minutes – meaning that during this period, at least one block will be fully hashed and a coin mined – and a hash tried on the block over and over until a unique hash specific to the bock was developed. However, in cases where this block would not have completed the hashing process, then an adjustment was made to it so as to ensure its complete hashing actually took place.

Given that this hash is tailored to the entire block, the idea as to how the different transactions within the block are maintained by the system often comes to question. To answer it, it is important to understand a different structure: the Merkle tree structure.

The Merkle tree brings a new twist to the hashing process. The ideology of the tree stems from the fact that the different transactions within the block – leaves – are themselves hashed and that the eventual result is the final hash resulting from both the transactions' hashes as well as the entire block's hashes – the root. This system ensures that all the transactions within the chain are maintained safely within the block. With this system in place, the only way for an attacker to change a transaction in the system would be for them to complete a hash of all transactions within that block as well as all which succeeded that block while at the same time maintaining a higher computational power than the system's users. This is impractical in reality and, as earlier stated, is the reason why Bitcoin is regarded safe within itself.

2.2.2.3. Bitcoin Mining: Difficulty

The mining of Bitcoin was initially designed to be done using the power from the central processing units (CPUs). In the earlier days, there were few people mining the cryptocurrency while at the same time only few transactions taking place during the period. As such, the hashing power which was required to run the network was quite minimal.

Over time, however, both the network users – leading to a higher number of transactions using Bitcoin – and number of miners grew. This is exemplified by the fact that the number of Bitcoin wallets kept growing over time, rising from just over 3.17 million back in the first quarter of 2015 to the over 21.5 million user wallets which were recorded in the fourth quarter of 2017. This led to the number of transactions during these periods rising from just over 85,000 transactions per day to nearly 200,000 transactions per day over the first quarter of 2015 to the fourth quarter of 2017 respectively.

Furthermore, the number of miners also rose during this period from the under 5,000 miners recorded back in 2013 to the over 100,000 recorded in 2017 – with the expected number of miners rising as the price of Bitcoin rises. This alluded to an increasing demand for the cryptocurrency both for the purpose of transactions as well as from the miners.

Such an increase in the number of miners, though welcome by the system as a way to enhance its security through an increase in the nodes, led to increased competition within the network. Over time, it became clearer that Central Processing Units (CPUs) were becoming obsolete in this mining process, leading to the shift towards Graphical Processing Units (GPUs). These complex processors were mainly used within the gaming world where faster processing power was required for rendering purposes. However, as with CPUs, the use of GPUs for mining purposes was quickly replaced by FPGAs (Field-Programmable Gate Arrays) and finally by ASICs (Application-Specific Integrated Circuits).

The entry of each new technology to the system was pivotal to the increased difficulty in the system's hashing. This figure which is computed using the tera hashes per second (TH/s) – easier defined as trillions of hashes per second – has been rising constantly through the years.

As at 2013 (during the period where CPUs completed the hashing process), the figure stood at 21 TH/s and rose to nearly 80,000 TH/s in mid-2014 (during the period where GPUs completed the hashing process). As at the end of January 2018, the figure had skyrocketed to over 21.6 million TH/s, a factor which alludes to the difficulty which has been brought about by the entry of Application-Specific Integrated Circuits into the mining space.

With the exponential increase in the hashing power required by the system came a new factor: the costs of mining kept rising. The key driver of this cost was the electricity costs which miners had to incur. This cost would further be exacerbated by the high price of purchasing Application-Specific Integrated Circuits. Miners therefore needed to be compensated for their role in keeping the system in its safe state and this led Satoshi to come up with a reward system.

2.2.2.4. Bitcoin Mining: Payoff

The difficulty in the hash rate was not the only problem that rocked cryptocurrency miners as they were also faced with a reducing Bitcoin reward for their mining role. Satoshi set up the reward algorithm in a manner that postulated that with the increase in the number of blocks released into the market – therefore the number of coins released – came the increase in difficulty in obtaining the cryptocurrency.

The reward scheme was set up in such a way initially, 50 Bitcoins would be distributed to the network with each block that was accepted. This meant that early adopters of the cryptocurrency benefited from having a higher reward for their work. However, this reward was meant to keep reducing over time. Over the first 210,000 blocks, it would be maintained at 50 Bitcoins per block but this figure would keep falling by half for every new 210,000 blocks – therefore between 210,000 blocks and 420,000 blocks the number of Bitcoins produced per block would reduce to 25 and reduce further to 12.5 between 420,000 blocks and 630,000 blocks and so on.

This payoff mechanism was meant to ensure that the cap for Bitcoins would be held at 21 million. As such, the number of Bitcoins released to the system would fall by a reducing balance over time. As at February 2018, the figure stood at 12.5 Bitcoins per block and is expected to half later in 2021.

Going forward, Satoshi also accounted for the fact that given the number of Bitcoins was had a cap, once all Bitcoins were distributed, it would be impossible for miners to benefit from the rising value of the coin. As such, they came up with an elaborate measure for this whereby the miners would be apportioned a percentage of the fees associated with carrying out transactions using the Bitcoin system. Given that the transactions were also on the rise, it was clear that the miners would need this system in future.

2.2.3. Bitcoin and Privacy

The growing size of the blockchain and the increased network size, despite having their perks, ended up having its downside. The main among this was on the reduced bandwidth within the network – as each node is doing a similar thing with the others – thus leading to a bottleneck in the network's scalability.

Bitcoin, courtesy of the above, would take a long period to accept, record and complete the transaction as it had to be accepted by the network as well as go through different roll-back problems that need to take shape. As such, after taking about 10 minutes to accept the transaction, it would take longer for it to reflect in the recipient's wallet, making scalability a problem. Despite this being a problem, the time taken was still shorter than it took for other traditional methods such as cheques which took about 2 days to clear.

Over time, courtesy of its advantages as well as its first mover advantage, Bitcoin has come to be accepted as a payment mechanism by many of its holders. This, however, has not stopped developers from noticing certain drawbacks akin to Bitcoin and working towards solving them.

One of these drawbacks is in anonymity (discussed later) and this is where Monero comes in.

3. Monero

3.1. Introduction

The evolution of cryptocurrencies has come a long way and with it has come a proliferation in the number of cryptocurrencies. Over the year ended December 2017, there was a surge in the number of Initial Coin Offerings (ICOs) in the market with the number rising from about 50 in 2016 to over 200 during the 2017 period.

Over time, it has become clearer to developers that they needed to differentiate themselves from other players within the market. Therefore, developers have decided to find different ways of creating their own niche within this space. This has led to different cryptocurrencies being formed in a bid to solve different global problems. Currently, cryptocurrencies have been tailored towards solving specific problems with cryptocurrencies being developed to solve education sector flaws, energy sector flaws and so on. Moreover, other have been tailored towards solving some of the problems akin to the initial blockchain architecture such as scalability, security or privacy. Such coins are tailored towards specific problems and their solutions developed to solve for them.

An exemplar of such a coin is Monero, a rising cryptocurrency which was developed to cater to cryptocurrency users who had one need, privacy.

3.2. History

Monero's history dates back to 18th April 2014 when the coin was launched to the Bitcoin talk platform by a person with the pseudonym 'thankful_for_today'. Back then, its name was BitMonero, a name which would later change to Monero about five days later. Prior to this, however, it is said that the underlying protocol on which it is based – the CryptoNote protocol – was originally launched by an author by the pseudonym Nicolas van Saberhagen.

During its creation, developers had one idea in mind: the promotion of privacy. This coin, unlike other cryptocurrencies, was developed with the sole interest of ensuring that it served a segment within the business community that did not wish to have their records go public. This included institutions such as banks as well as other financial institutions which have a duty of confidentiality to their clients or other private corporations which are not mandated to store their records publicly and prefer to keep these records private.

The talk on privacy was, however, both its strong suit and its detriment.

The coin's acceptance grew quickly courtesy of its applicability within the dark web – a section of the web which is uncontrolled and in which criminals easily find access to some of their weapons as well as other immoral services (thus dark web) and can only be accessed through specific web applications. As early as 2016, only two years after its launch, the cryptocurrency was being used by AlphaBay, a market within the dark web community. Shortly after the realization, the site was closed by law enforcement.

It is postulated by some that the reason behind the rise of Monero was its favouritism by illegal traders and criminals who preferred to remain anonymous during such trades or activities (as shown by its increased used within the AlphaBay network). However, the cryptocurrency builds its own case by stating that the good from its use within financial and other private institutions by far outweighs the bad that is presented to the world on the demerits of the cryptocurrency.

While building on its name and its key attribute, the cryptocurrency has grown to become one of the largest in the market – based on market capitalization statistics – and stands at twelfth position as at February 2018.

3.3. Developmental Cornerstones

Monero was formed on four key pillars: privacy, security, intractability and fungibility. All these (except security), according to the developers, were meant to be additions to the already existing cryptocurrency frameworks such as decentralization, scalability and proof-of-work, all which the cryptocurrency meets. As stated, given that Monero used a similar framework as did Bitcoin, the same security options akin to other blockchain users were available for them.

However, it is when we get to the other pillars that we establish the benefits of Monero.

3.3.1. Ring Signatures

First in on privacy where Monero went ahead to bring to the market a novel idea, the ring signatures.

This novel technology was developed by Ron Rivest, Adi Shamir, and Yael Tauman back in 2001 in a bid to counter the negative implications of the lack of privacy which surrounded cryptographic algorithms back then. Advancements to this initial idea were then made by Fujisaki and Suzuki and these formed the basis for the new ring signatures system.

Ring signatures are established by mixing the keys – private or public – from different transactions within a group thus ensuring that individuals outside of these transactions cannot identify the initiator or recipient of the funds from a specific transaction. The architecture of this system was the basis on which the name ring signatures was formed as it was designed in such a way that the keys of the initiator or recipient were mixed in a ring-like fashion (given that they were in a group). This, tied with the fact that real identities are obscured via blockchain technology, means that the transactions are in turn untraceable – a factor which made Monero seem like a safe haven for criminals.

These two differ significantly from Bitcoin and other cryptocurrencies which stocks to the address provided so as to transfer the funds from one account to another and despite there being no link between the account holder and their address, individuals can track back a specific set of transactions meticulously back to a specific individual once their address comes to light.

At this time, however, Monero's developers had been made aware of the coin's reputation as being a black-market coin, one meant to ensure the security of criminals. They therefore made adjustments to their platform.

3.3.2. Spend and View Keys

Monero is termed by many as being opaquely-transparent. Given that most of Monero's users were institutions or individuals operating legally within their respective countries, it was only a matter of time before the government or other regulatory bodies begun looking into some of their documents. With Monero being an opaque cryptocurrency, such an exercise would have been deemed impossible, a factor which would have been detrimental for the cryptocurrency.

As such, the developers coined a way in which the cryptocurrency's transparency would be achieved. This was through the issuance of a spend and view key.

The spend key, the users can spend. It was quite similar to any other cryptocurrency key as its role was to ensure that the user could conduct their transactions as is the case for all cryptocurrencies. However, it was in the next key that transparency was achieved.

The view key allowed the users to allow other parties to view the transactions which they take part. It serves as some type of access for authorized users only into an individual's transactional history on Monero. Through this, the user is in total control of their account and can decide when they wish to take whichever action. This is especially beneficial for financial institutions which can use the view key to provide access to auditors or regulators during audit periods or tax filing periods respectively

3.3.3. Fungibility

Finally came fungibility – the ability of one coin to be equivocated for another with the same value as itself.

To give this some context, Bitcoin has its coins tied to the addresses which they have gone through. Due to this, once these coins have moved from one account to the next, they store the codes for the accounts through which they moved. As such, an individual can decide not to accept coins from certain accounts such as those which have been seen to conduct illegal trades or crime – this is not necessarily a bad thing as it may alleviate such crimes, however, if the previous owner of the coin had no knowledge that their coin had been used for such activities, this places them at a disadvantage.

Fungibility comes to solve for this by ensuring that any trader can accept any coins as their value is similar. As such, these coins can be equivocated for each other and, as a result of the coins' lack of traceability, no one can pinpoint a single coin as is the case with Bitcoin.

3.4. Mining Architecture

All the above developments have driven Monero to its success. The coin has solved quite a number of problems akin to the cryptocurrency space in its own fashion. Currently, its developers seem to have clearly cut out their niche and focused their efforts at satisfying their customers.

Despite this being so, it is also important to cater to the needs of the individuals keeping the system safe. In this section, we thus look at Monero's mining process.

3.4.1. History

Satoshi's initial goal was for there to be an elaborate 'one-CPU-one-vote' system in cryptocurrencies. Such a system would ensure that all nodes within the system had equal rights in governing the system and this would ensure that the entire system was fully decentralized. However, this was curtailed by the emergence of more sophisticated machines such as Application-Specific Integrated Circuits.

Such machines brought about competition with the then popular Central Processing Unit mining method. With their processing power being unequalled, miners had to gather resources and purchase the expensive equipment in order to profitably continue with the mining process. This in turn was against the very goal set out by Satoshi as individuals with more resources had more power than those with less. This meant that if individuals with resources purchased more of the ASICs, they would then have more power to govern the system.

Developers at Monero realized this significant flaw within the Bitcoin architecture and implemented a solution to it, the CryptoNote protocol.

3.4.2. CryptoNote

The CryptoNote protocol came to provide the solution to this problem.

Similar to the SHA-256 algorithm which is present in most cryptocurrencies, CryptoNote employs a proof-of-work system whereby nodes within the system have to take part in the hashing process for the reward-based system to hold. However, that is as far as their similarities go.

CryptoNote then diverges into ensuring some form of equity among miners by employing a memory bound function. This function bases the time to a solution on the amount of memory deemed necessary for that specific problem to be solved. This is unlike the CPU bound function whereby the processing power is the variable assessed in determining the time necessary to complete the hashing process.

The use of the memory bound function removes the use of processors with higher computing power – courtesy of the pipeline[5] effect – from the equation. As a result, machines using pipelined systems are eliminated from this, leaving only Central Processing Units – x86 and upwards – and Graphics Processing Units in the mining space.

Through this, the system solved one of the major flaws with many cryptocurrency mining systems and gave miners a level playing field on which to operate. CryptoNote therefore served as a major plus to miners.

---

[5] The pipeline effect (instruction pipelining) occurs when instructions sent to a processor are divided into smaller sequential steps from which the processor can execute them. This means that the processor can, instead of completing a transaction as a whole then moving to the next transaction, execute bits of instructions in parallel therefore allowing it to complete more instructions much quicker and in a much more efficient manner. This, however, has a negative effect on the response time of the software (increases latency).

4. The Battle of the Cryptocurrencies

4.1. Behind the Battle

The previous chapters have spoken to all the benefits and drawbacks of the two cryptocurrencies. It is clear that they (cryptocurrencies) have brought to the world great solutions not only their form but also in how they operate. These currencies have brought with them a revolution to the modern economics age by both changing the dynamics of most economics concept – as we will see in the use of cryptocurrencies as a store of value later in this book – as well as integrating currencies with technology. This presents a new age to users of money as well as its regulators as Central Banks are now being made more aware of this development and its role in the world.

This being said, these cryptocurrencies have also been seen to be dynamic in the solutions they have brought to the market. Starting with their forerunner, Bitcoin, these currencies have been built on different systems. The diversity in their architecture is also palpable and people attribute this to the different solutions they bring to the market. These differences have both their positives and drawbacks – as this concept is still in its development stage and still undergoing major transformations – but on the overall, they are a step in the positive direction.

Despite this, it is important to critique some of these differences so as to address especially the drawbacks to the system. Here, we the two coins are assessed based on their characteristics and the solutions to some of their drawbacks given.

4.2. Bitcoin Versus Monero

It is important to start by stating that both coins have one fundamental role, to act as a medium of exchange. Over time, it is becoming increasingly clear both to governments and to their citizens that cryptocurrencies are playing this role as effectively as was the case in the traditional system.

However, it is in playing this role that we find the first drawback to the two cryptocurrencies.

4.2.1. Scalability

Both cryptocurrencies are quite slow in their transaction times. It takes over 20 minutes for both of the cryptocurrencies to reflect that a transaction has been undertaken in the system, a factor which would have negative effects on business worldwide.

The current business environment has been based on the fast and efficient systems of service providers. This is clear to any user who has used the services of companies such as Visa or Mastercard as these companies' complete transactions over a period of seconds. Users merely need to swipe their card and are sure that the receiver will receive the money shortly after and this has made business around the globe much faster.

This explains why users having to wait over 30 minutes for a transaction to be verified by a system would be setting the world of business back by over a decade. Both coins are therefore poorer at accomplishing this role than the traditional system. Let us understand how.

Bitcoin's system takes about 10 minutes to mine a coin, meaning that a block is created every ten minutes. Given that every transaction is recorded in the ledger after the block has been mined, it would take about 10 minutes for a single transaction to be recorded on the ledger. However, it does not end here as the wallet must show that this transaction has been completed and this is where it takes time.

It takes another thirty to forty-five minutes after the first ten minutes for a transaction to be deemed complete at which period the confirmation to the wallets of the recipient of the coin receive the notice of completion of this transaction. in short, Bitcoin users need to wait in a line at a grocery store for forty-five minutes for their payment to reflect in the store's system before they can leave during which period a credit card user has already made a meal back home.

This is not the case for Bitcoin alone as Monero in turn takes nearly four minutes for a transaction to be recorded and about 26 minutes for confirmations to be sent on the different wallets.

The two situations above stem from one problem which affects all cryptocurrencies: scalability[6]. Given that the transaction processing capacity of the cryptocurrency network is limited by the average block creation time – which stands at about 10 minutes for Bitcoin and just over two minutes for Monero – and the block sizes are limited, the network's throughput is generally limited. Therefore, the transaction processing capacity is limited to a specific number of transactions per unit time.

The scalability problem is one which affects the above cryptocurrencies significantly and one which, despite the benefits of the blockchain network, has led to individuals and entities not accepting these cryptocurrencies. With players such as fast food networks receiving millions in revenue from the thousands of transactions daily, it would be hard to verify these transactions hours after they occurred.

As such, despite Monero being a much better cryptocurrency on this segment – based on the higher transaction speed – both of these cryptocurrencies need to do a lot before they receive the acceptance that service providers such as Visa receive.

---

[6] The scalability problem refers to the limits on the amount of transactions the cryptocurrency network can process. It is a consequence of the fact that records (known as blocks) in the blockchain are limited in size and frequency. These blocks include the transactions on the cryptocurrency network.

4.2.2. Privacy

As previously alluded to, Monero was created so as to overcome one key drawback of Bitcoin: its lack of privacy.

Through the use of ring signatures and fungibility, Monero has ensured that neither can a user's address be viewed or tracked by another user on the platform and that the amounts transferred by a user can also not be tracked by others. This solves a recurring problem with Bitcoin whereby users can refuse to accept coins tied to certain accounts – mostly accounts with ties to criminal activity.

This keenness to privacy has brought about Monero's fondness among certain players within the cryptocurrency space. It is expected to play a major role in the future of Monero.

The Better Coin

With the above in mind, it is quite visible that Monero came to solve for the drawbacks of Bitcoin. The discussion on which of the two reigns superior has yet to be exhausted as these boils down mostly to preference.

Despite there seeming to be an objective way to review cryptocurrencies, most individuals simply choose Monero due to their preference for anonymity. However, if analysed, among the key things to look at would be the coin's acceptability (as shown by the size of their user base), how many coins are already distributed[7], the team behind its development as well as the market it is targeting.

On all of the above, both coins perform quite well despite Bitcoin overshadowing Monero in terms of its acceptability. However, it is also important to acknowledge that both cryptocurrencies bring a lot to the table and that their functionality is beneficial to the financial community.

---

[7] The number of distributed coins gives one an idea on how large a share price surge would affect the coin. Coins with much lower distribution end up benefiting from having a lower supply therefore a much larger demand and finally a much higher price in contrast to those with a much higher distribution.

5. How to buy?

The above cryptocurrencies are mostly purchased through different exchanges. An advantage they have is that due to their large market capitalization therefore reputation within the market, it is easy to purchase them unlike other smaller alt coins.

Bitcoin has the advantage of being available on every exchange across the globe. However, the easiest platforms to buy it are Coinbase and CoinMama. Coinbase especially was formed back in 2011 by two developers, Brian Armstrong and Fred Ehrsam after which it quickly grew into one of the largest exchanges in the world. Currently, it operates in over 32 countries in the world and has morphed to incorporate a cryptocurrency application in the process. To run an account, one needs to register on the site with authentic identification documents and in order to trade, there are fees which must be paid.

The site has currently incorporated a vault which is a safe place to store one's coins. Through this, it is trying to ensure that they beef up security on their platform. The platform ensures that one can sign up either as an individual or as a group after which they receive services such as a 48-hour withdrawal period from which they can cancel the withdrawal and group authentication, all in a bid to boost security.

For Monero, there are only but a few exchanges that allow it to be traded. These exchanges include Poloniex, Bittrex, Shapeshift, Bitfinex and Changelly.

Of all the above, Shapeshift is the one exchange that does not require the user to include their details, rather, they merely need to include the account they are transferring their coins from or to.

With its fees differing between cryptocurrencies, it serves as one of the best platforms for individuals to obtain different cryptocurrencies without having to register. Furthermore, of all the exchanges detailed, it is the one exchange which operates across the globe – with the exception of North Korea and New York (due to the Bitfinex laws within the state).

With this, we presume that investors will find it easy to invest in either of the above cryptocurrencies and benefit from these investments courtesy of a high return on them.

6. Storing Cryptocurrencies

6.1. Underlying Economics

Money serves different functions in the human life. Primarily, it is used as a measure of payment therefore used in facilitating trade between different parties. Over time, however, the functions of money kept evolving and other roles were added on.

One key role courtesy of this morphosis was the role of money as a store of wealth. People begun using money as an asset, one which would be held for long period and used to store the value the money had over long periods. Innately, money acted in the same capacity as shares or commodities since people could now hold it for longer periods. This role was driven by a different economic factor: interest[8] rates.

However, there was one fear inherent in this function: people could only hold money as a store of value if the inflation[9] rate in the economy was low. If this rate kept rising, money holders were seen to be losing value as their money could only buy a

---

[8] Interest rate is the amount of return one earns on saving their money rather than using it for consumption – the technical explanation for this is that interest rates serve as a return to compensate the holder of money for foregoing current consumption for future consumption.

[9] Inflation is a term used in economics to define the deterioration in the purchasing power of money. It is computed by assessing the amount of goods an individual could buy at a certain historical period in time versus how much they can buy at present. On the overall, economists believe that a little inflation is necessary in an economy as it acts as an incentive for producers to keep producing goods or rendering services, however, once inflation rises above set targets, it begins to have negative implications on the economy, especially on poor people who cannot afford the now expensive gods.

little amount of goods at that period as compared to what it could previously buy. This was mainly because during periods of high inflation the interest rate earned from saving money is way lower than the loss in the value of money courtesy of the high inflation, necessitating people to consume more. Given this, individuals needed to be kept in the know on the inflation rates in a country and with the evolution of governments and Central Banks, this became a key concern for them as the realization that it tied to other economic factors became clearer.

In their formation, cryptocurrencies factored in the above economic characteristics of money and made significant changes to them. First, the finite nature of cryptocurrencies would see their value rise over time, meaning that the holders of these currencies were being compensated for holding them through time.

Interest rates are therefore taken out of the equation as individuals holding these cryptocurrencies is innately self-paying. Moreover, once an individual received a loan using cryptocurrencies, the interest they paid out on them would keep rising over time, leading the loan to become unpayable. On to inflation, cryptocurrencies have come up with fixed inflation rates governing the entire system. These rates are based on how many cryptocurrencies are released to the world over a particular period of time. Developers have made it a priority to limit this number so as to ensure that people benefit from low inflation.

This clearly shows the ideology behind holding cryptocurrencies: consistency in purchasing power. As such, holding cryptocurrencies will, in future, be driven primarily by the need to gain from their rising value. Their finite nature acts as a demand-driver, ensuring that individuals continuously benefit from a system which does not merely hurt the poor – due to the high inflation rates (as well as hyper-inflation in some cases) which characterized the old system – while making the rich richer – due to the high interest rates the rich received during periods of high inflation.

Despite all this, cryptocurrencies faced one key hurdle: how could a digital currency which was new to the market and decentralized be stored? At this time, these currencies were prone to hacking from attackers and this only became worse after their increase in value was seen by the market. Such attacks necessitated developers to come together and develop more secure methods of storing these currencies. These methods are discussed in the next section.

6.2. The Store of Value: Cryptocurrency Wallets

Cryptocurrency wallets can be broken down into five: desktop wallets, online wallets, hardware wallets, paper wallets and mobile wallets. As with the name, these wallets are operated on the different platforms encompassed in the name therein.

Desktop wallets were the first type of wallets created with their forerunner, Bitcoin Core, being the first of this kind. Back then, these wallets were made to serve the purpose of storage only. However, with time, their purpose was augmented to suit different clientele such as those who preferred advanced security or anonymity got to get their own different wallets. Such include Armory and Electrum.

With time, however, convenience came into play as people needed to have their wallets with them more often so as to allow for them to pay for some of their goods and services while on the road, leading to the creation of mobile wallets. These wallets were meant to purely support payments using this cryptocurrency. Unlike other full bitcoin clients – who had to download the entire blockchain framework – these run on a portion of this framework and have the notion of simplified payment verification behind their formation.

The online wallet came by default courtesy of Bitcoin being a digital currency. They provided online service to clients with their personal information being stored on a company's server. However, this was in turn a drawback, the cryptocurrencies were meant to give the control to the holder and not to an entity storing the holder's information. Be though this the case, they have served the purpose of ensuring people are connected to the cryptocurrency space. Such platforms include sites like Coinbase or Blockchain.info.

The next two wallets came to add on to the security features of Bitcoin wallets. They represent a form of storage known as cold storage – this is where the holder of Bitcoin does not wish to keep their money online or on any server therefore keeps it as 'its raw form of currency': either as the physical coin, paper or on a hardware device.

First is the paper wallet. This wallet serves as the cheapest method of storing Bitcoin. It comes with two QR codes on its surface enabling the use and receipt of the cryptocurrency. Furthermore, given that the Bitcoin keys – the private codes that enable transactions to be carried out – are stored on the paper rather than online, the wallet serves as a much safer method of storage as it is not prone to hacking as with other software-based wallets.

This being said, let us get to the most advanced of these wallets: the hardware wallet.

Hardware wallets are physical gadgets, similar to mobile phones, which are dedicated to Bitcoin. They serve as holders of the electronic keys of the cryptocurrency and are therefore used to facilitate payment.

Unlike other wallets, you actually have to pay a significant sum of money to acquire this wallet with some going as high as $240. This is especially so because of the fact that they are limited in supply – very limited supply versus higher demand causes prices to go up. However, with such a price, there must be value and this is what these wallets offer.

The main wallets in this category include Ledger Nano, SatoshiLabs Trezor and KeepKey with other advancements in this space having already been made such as Boinym's heartbeat sensing wallet which uses the rhythm of the heartbeat for security purposes.

Of all the above, hardware wallets (cold storage systems) are preferred as unlike other wallets, they are not prone to hacking and are therefore safe. For the case of Bitcoin and Monero, similar advice is offered.

Given the value of the cryptocurrency and the resources necessary to obtain them, it is prudent for the user to avoid loss of the same. Therefore, any system that provides higher security to the user is preferred in this case, making the hardware wallets preferable. However, if one cannot buy these wallets, they can generate their own paper wallets for either Bitcoin or Monero. Both of these wallets are tamper-proof and have higher security as they are not prone to hacking as is the case for online storages.

Before investing

Disclaimer: This book does not supersede any financial advice given by a financial analyst, rather serves merely as an information toolkit that improves the reader's knowledge of the two cryptocurrencies. Investing in cryptocurrencies is risky and you can lose some or all your money in the process.

Before investing, readers need to understand the asset they are investing in innately. First, they need to and must carry out due diligence before investing.

6.3. Due Diligence

Due diligence is a process whereby the investor goes thorough the statements, processes and premises of the entity they wish to invest in for the investor to validate that what has been reported by the company in their statements is actually true. This is a process which may take time, however, most of it has been made easy by the strict laws that require disclosures and periodic releases of information to the public. In case you are not investing in a public company, you may be required to actually visit the premises of the entity as you conduct your due diligence as most of their information is held privately.

The need for due diligence cannot be underscored further as it is the one measure meant to ensure that you are not conned off of your money by unscrupulous individuals.

6.4. Term and Tools of Trade

Second, the trader will need to define the term of their trades – short-term or long-term – and devise different methods of assessing their asset prices over that term.

To do this, tools such as technical tools[10] and fundamental tools[11] exist. These tools help one understand different facets of the asset's price as well as its drivers. It is also important to point out that in most cases, technical tools are used by short-term traders (such as day-traders) while fundamental analysis ends up being used by long-term traders – mainly because they forecast the time before they recoup their investment and this will generally take more than one year or a minimum of six months.

6.5. Data Analysis

Despite analysis tools playing a key role in investments, the data used in the analysis plays a more pivotal role. As per the phrase 'garbage in garbage out', if the data used for analysis is bad, everything about the entire process follows suit making any conclusions arrived at to be erroneous. Investors should take

---

[10] Technical analysis is based on one's analysis of asset price movement patterns whereby the trader expects that the price patterns will recur and they will capitalize on them. In order to do this, different technical tools have been developed such as the Moving Average Convergence Divergence (MACD), Bollinger Bands, Relative Strength Index (RSI) etc.

[11] Fundamental analysis is based on the analysis of the asset's revenue, cash flow and risk drivers. Here, the financial statements are analyzed with an incline towards understanding the strength of their books and how risky these books are after which forecasts are made and based on the output from these, investments too are made.

time and find the best data for use in their analysis as it drives the conclusions reached upon.

One trusted site that is sure to deliver high quality data on cryptocurrencies is Kaggle.

Kaggle, a site formed by developers, has been at the forefront of storing cryptocurrency data. The data which has been made publicly available – and can be accessed on https://www.kaggle.com/jessevent/all-crypto-currencies/data – will be pivotal in ensuring that one easily carries out and completes their data analysis process.

6.6. Trading Strategies

Now that we have completed our analysis, it is important for the reader to understand how to trade. Trading in cryptocurrencies differs from most other trades in that the volatility[12] in this market is quite high.

This therefore makes trading in cryptocurrencies riskier – as a result of higher volatility. Investors have therefore tried to combat this risk by coming up with newer strategies. One such strategy is the dollar-cost averaging strategy.

This strategy entails the investor investing smaller fixed amounts in an investment over different time periods. This

---

[12] Volatility in finance refers to the changes experienced in the asset prices over a particular time. If the prices are seen to be changing very fast and over very high ranges, it is said that the asset's price is more volatile while if the price remains within certain low or expected boundaries, it is more volatile.

allows them to schedule their investments slowly over time with investors buying more when the prices of the asset are lower and more when they are higher. As a result, their average purchase price of the asset stands to be lower than it would have been if they invested the entire amount at the previous higher price.

In the case of cryptocurrencies, it would be advisable to buy Bitcoin or Monero at a lower price – given the volatility of the assets, this price may fall or rise quickly over a short period of time – and hold them over time as this price rises. If their average price is lower, the gains accrued to this investor would be quite high, making them smart investors in the long run.

Another important strategy is to ensure one understands the coin's market capitalization[13]. While many people focus on the price of the coin – with the hope of purchasing it at a very low price of below $1 and selling it at a high price so as to maximize on the gains – the cryptocurrency space requires an analysis of the market capitalization. Generally, the market capitalization is a better indicator as to how far upwards a coin's price can rise. Cryptocurrencies with high market capitalization allude to one thing: the fact that the market has invested significantly in them and is still demanding more of the coin means that they have a higher belief in the future of the coin. This means that it is more trusted thus making it more difficult for the coin to fall in future.

---

[13] Market capitalization is defined as the market value of an asset. Its value is derived by multiplying the price of the asset by the total volume of the asset traded in the market. In the case of cryptocurrencies, the total volume is the number of coins in circulation.

Once these coins are purchased, it will be important to diversify[14]. Diversification ensures that the investor will not lose their money in case of a collapse in the market therefore catering to the risk of correlation between risk factors in different industries. As with any asset, it is important for investors to put some of their money in Bitcoin or Monero while putting some other money in other assets which are uncorrelated or negatively correlated with cryptocurrencies – such as bonds or gold. Through this, even during a period of downturn in cryptocurrencies, the investor will have mitigated the effect of this downturn on their portfolio as it will be offset by the upturn in the uncorrelated or negatively correlated asset.

Finally, investor would benefit from learning that the best time to invest in a cryptocurrency is now. Given that the prices of assets eventually end up rising, investing early in these assets is a sure way of benefiting from this price increases. This is especially so for the cryptocurrency market as its market capitalization has been rising at a drastic rate – having risen from $5.1 billion in the beginning of 2015 to $473 billion in the beginning of 2018. Such benefits, in the long run, are expected to accrue investors who put their money within this space.

---

[14] Diversification is a finance concept that speaks to an investor not 'putting all their eggs in one basket'. Rather, investors are advised to put different percentages of their investments in different assets so as to ensure that they do not lose all their money in case of a collapse in a given sector in the market.

Eventually, all the strategies employed will be based on the same trading concept, buy low and sell high. As such, investors would be prudent to read a lot more on different investment strategies – similar to the dollar-cost averaging strategy – so as to gain more solid grounding in the investment field.

6.7. Risk-Reward and Emotions

Once the above two are done and the investor is comfortable of the risk-reward trade-off they expect, they can invest their money. There are, however, still some things they need to be weary of or avoid.

Investors need to alleviate their emotions from their investments. Given that investment has a personal feel to it as it directly impacts the money we have, this becomes a difficult thing to do. However, if an investor pegs their emotions to their investments, they end up being biased and making irrational investment decisions in the process. Second it for investors to beware of pump and dump strategies where individuals come together and continuously buy an asset in order to hike its price before dumping the asset to the market.

This is the reason why due diligence and valuation are ever-so important to investors as they help them find out the intrinsic value of an asset thus ensure that they can spot such a market movement as it occurs.

Finally, given that any asset is affected by information from countries and other regulatory bodies – especially for cryptocurrencies which are new to the market thus prone to regulatory changes by countries across the globe – it is important to follow global news. This will inform most of the decisions the investor makes and give them an understanding – with time – of how different news events will affect the movement in the prices of a cryptocurrency.

Having understood this, investors can now begin to look into different investment options and evaluate their feasibility.

7. Epilogue

It is clear that they (cryptocurrencies) have brought to the world great solutions not only their form but also in how they operate. These currencies have brought with them a revolution to the modern economics age by both changing the dynamics of most economics concept as well as integrating currencies with technology. This presents a new age to users of money as well as its regulators as Central Banks are now being made more aware of this development and its role in the world.

These forms of currency have brought promise and hope to individuals worldwide; their promises embedded in words such as decentralization – the elimination of third parties such as banks from the transaction table –, low to zero transaction costs, high speed transactions and high security. Most people have only been made aware of the above strengths akin to the new technology.

Over time, the world edges closer to their acceptance as we look forward to a cryptocurrency filled and driven world.

8. Conclusion

Thank you once again for buying this book.

Over the course of this book, we have sought to ensure that the reader has the full gist of the cryptocurrency space. We expect that it will provide them with an ample grounding from which they can make decisions regarding this space.

We expect to keep updating readers with more content as it arises and would like to request you to subscribe to the email list on

http://www.aboutcryptocurrencies.net/

Once done, you will receive an email with a **free** ebook and continuous updates on developments within this space. You will also have the opportunity to receive all my future crypto currency books for free.

If you enjoyed this book, kindly leave a review on Amazon. These reviews will help better your experience in future publications. In order to review the book, click here.

We hope you had a good read. All the best in your cryptocurrency investment endeavours.

Johan von Amsterdam

www.ingramcontent.com/pod-product-compliance
Lightning Source LLC
Chambersburg PA
CBHW030047230526
45471CB00003B/984